With
love
to
Paul
and
to
Philip

ISBN 0-590-16241-1

12 11 10 9 8 7 6 5 4 3 2   1/0

Printed in the U.S.A.   08

First Scholastic printing, November 1996

Behind the Mask

A Book About Prepositions

Written and illustrated by
RUTH HELLER

SCHOLASTIC INC.
New York   Toronto   London   Auckland   Sydney

Of PREPOSITIONS have no fear. They help to make directions clear.

beyond
this
green,
reptilian
beast . . .
past its hungry,
gaping
mouth . . .

veer directly . . .

to the south,
toward a place
where mermaids flock
upon,
beside,
and **near** a rock.

One
hundred
twenty
paces
west . . .
the
treasure
lies
inside
this
chest.

PREPOSITIONS
are the best!

They're never alone.
They're always
in phrases . . .   **behind**   the
                                                                 masks
                                                                 and . . .

through the mazes.

They almost always   start the phrase . . .

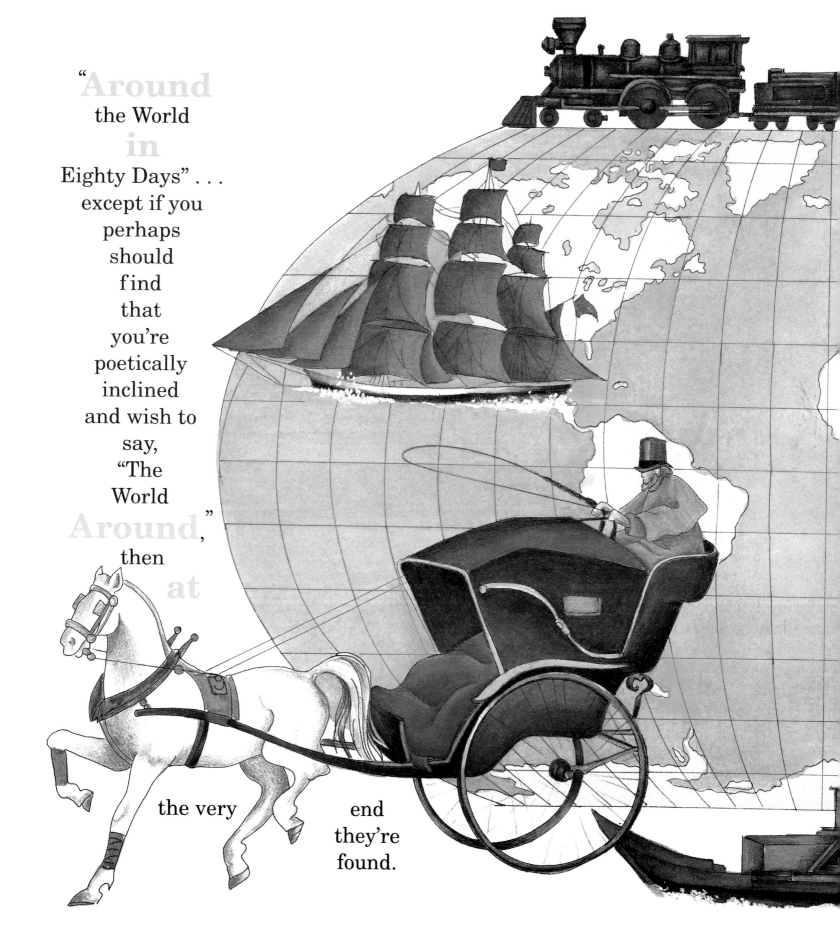

"Around the World in Eighty Days" . . . except if you perhaps should find that you're poetically inclined and wish to say, "The World Around," then at the very end they're found.

Of
PREPOSITIONS
have
no
fear.

In
phrases
only
they
appear.

So
if
a
word
upon
this
list
without
a
phrase
is
found . . .

about
above
across
after
against
along
amid
among
around
at

atop
before
behind
below
beneath
beside
besides
between
beyond
but

by
concerning
down
during
except
for
from
in
inside
into
like

near
of
off
on
onto
out
outside
over
past
regarding
since

through
throughout
to toward
under
underneath
until
unto
up upon
with
within
without

as when I say . . .

"Please step inside,
come in,
and
look around."
It's not a
PREPOSITION,
so
take a careful look.
It's
probably an
ADVERB
and is **in**
another
book.

So you will never be confused . . . here are some rules
that can be used.
The cow jumped

over

the

moon.

The
dish ran
away
with the spoon.
PREPOSITIONS tell you where.

They
tell you how . . .

and
when.
Please don't
wake us
until
ten.

Into
means
"to enter,"
and
that's the reason
why . . .
"Step into my parlor,"
said
the
spider
to the fly.

But if inside *already* is what you really mean . . .
then . . . eating bread and honey . . .

in
the parlor
is the queen.

Be angry **with** a person, but angry **at** a thing.
I'm angry **with** Jack
and
I'm angry **with** Jill . . .
but,
I'm angrier
still
at
the
pail
and
the
hill.

Between must be said when referring **to** two, and **among** when referring **to** more.

The ten is **between** the king and the queen . . .

and the five is **among** these four.

Say, " different **from**," not "different than."
Find the odd one if you can.

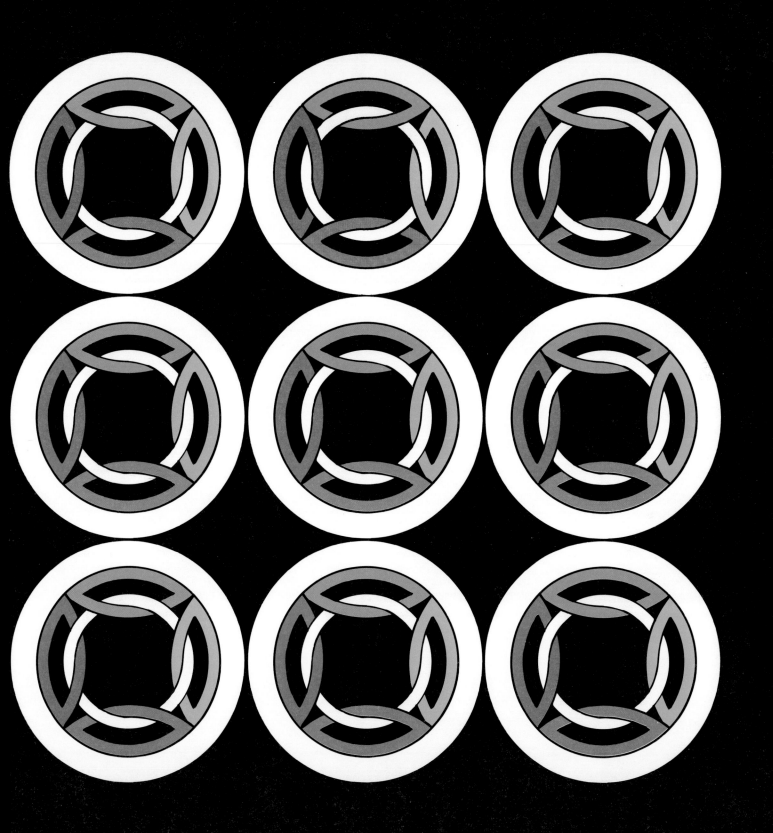

This is a test. . . . Which one is different **from** the rest?

And two PREPOSITIONS aren't better than one. . . .
Icarus flew **near**,
not near to,   the sun.

One is
enough . . .

to
tell
you
where.

They
fell
off,
but not
off of,

the red
rocking chair.

Despite what you have heard,

sometimes PREPOSITIONS can be more than

The deer is **in front of** the camel. . . .

The lion's **in back of** the hors

just one
word.

These are
PHRASAL
PREPOSITIONS

and . . .

here are more
of them, **of** course.

on account of
according to   as of   owing to
apart from   because of   in spite of
by means of   instead of   in regard to
in addition to   next to   in view of
as far as   out of   in place of

PREPOSITIONS, **in** this modern day,
at the end **of**
a sentence
are sometimes okay.
So it isn't an error . . . it isn't a sin
to say,
"It's the room that I was playing
in."
But those who are graced
with
impeccable taste
will insist upon saying,
"It is the room **in** which I was playing."